Soft

Gentle 8

---A Remembered Prose

James A. Hunter

outskirts
press

Soft And Gentle 8
—A Remembered Prose
All Rights Reserved.
Copyright © 2021 James A. Hunter
v2.0

Outskirts Press, Inc.
http://www.outskirtspress.com

ISBN: 978-1-9772-4579-3

Library of Congress Control Number: 2021914320

Outskirts Press and the "OP" logo
are trademarks belonging to Outskirts Press, Inc.

PRINTED IN THE UNITED STATES OF AMERICA

Use Your QR App
To Learn More Today

Dedicated to

My grandparents, John Anderson Hunter and Millie Francis (Sandlin) Hunter, who had the foresight and courage to purchase the farm on Pipe Creek over one hundred years ago. It provided a sense of independence to some of their descendants, enough to carry on in their footsteps. I hope that those following will ensure that the land stays in the family for another hundred years.

Foreword

This book is the eighth in the series of my writings entitled <u>Soft And Gentle—A Remembered Prose</u>. The pieces of work for this book were all written in 2016. Publication of my work always lags a little behind their writing because I like to give my pieces a little time to age. Hopefully, the aging gives me a different, better, perspective before final editing. By the time it leaves my hands, I have labored over it like the piece of love it is. I continue to write about the common, ordinary things in life that everyone can relate to.

Several pieces in each book of my work will contain pieces of nostalgia that go back to my childhood when times were more simple. Although one must somewhat change as the world changes, I believe in hanging onto good memories of the past. Even if the reader cannot totally relate to a piece, if I can take the reader back in time and make them feel as if they were there with me, then I have accomplished my purpose. Those from my generation should identify with most of those nostalgic pieces, and those of another generation may possibly better understand my generation.

Nature has always had a huge influence on my writing. Everything in nature is beautiful in its own way. It can be just as beautiful when eloquently described through the eyes of one who loves what they see. Nature has been a constant for me. It has always been there to inspire me, whether I am feeling up or down. When I am feeling up, it lifts me higher, and when I am feeling down, it lifts me back up. That recipe has always been effective for me.

This timeless work can be enjoyed a piece at a time, or all in one setting. Whichever way works for the reader, I hope that they enjoy this work that came straight from the heart.

James A. Hunter

Contents

Wildflower Off-Season

It does not need to be spring
before I am inspired enough
to pen about tiny wildflowers
peeping up from between
leaves in the wood,
because I have visited them
often enough in their season
to memorize their beauty
and carry it with me
throughout their off-season

Paths That Others Ignore

Many take the same path
over and over again
when traveling
to their destinations,
but I prefer to take
the paths that they ignore.
When traveling thereby,
I hunger to learn more
about people, places,
and things
all along its way,
and therefore be a vigilant,
observant participant in any
newly-discovered beauty

Tipping My Hat

The robin is so glad
to be about again
that she tells me
over and over.
I, glad to see her back
and wanting her to continue
spreading her gladness,
acknowledge her greetings
with a tip of my hat,
even if she realizes
that my selfish objective
is condescending
and for my own enjoyment

The Day's Tugging Issues

The day pulls at me
from several directions:
chores wait to be done,
repairs wait to be made,
errands wait to be run,
family waits to be called on,
explorations wait to gratify me,
the wood waits to soothe me,
bench-sitting waits to relax me,
and so on.
My instincts,
which have been
carefully developed over time,
tell me that I need to choose
those issues leaning toward work
rather than leisure.
I am inclined to redirect my focus
as I criticize the day
for being several hours short,
because lengthening the day
could have been a fair remedy
for most of these tugging issues

Glory Snows Of Old

The soft, quiet, wet, fluffy snows
that we used to have with regularity
were a time of celebration
for the children in my family.
Select hills of our farm
suddenly gained instant value,
and we sledded and played
until we could play no more;
then, we had snowball fights
until someone inevitably got hurt,
usually the youngest, yours truly.
As daylight faded,
we were satisfied that it had been
a perfect day to be a kid,
as we sat around the supper table
excitedly trading
our day's adventures and stories.
As evening finally came,
we would anticipate and prepare for
the most delightful indulgence of all—
ice cream made from fresh snow,
a perfect complement to our fun day

The Child Within Us

I have carefully guarded
the child within me,
so that I always have ample
to draw me closer
to the age
that I want to be,
and push me away
from the age
that I am,
and that suffices for me.
For anyone beginning
to feel a little too old,
finding the child
within themselves
may help to slow
the dreaded aging process

Birth Of The Tulip

On this mild day in April
when she can hardly bear
the wait any longer,
the tulip finally decides
that her time has arrived.
With all the might
that she can muster,
she sets her shoulders
to the soil above her
and begins her course
of emerging.
Alternating between
short, powerful heaves
and timely rest,
she finally succeeds
in pushing through
the stubborn soil
into open, refreshing
spring air,
setting the stage
for final progression
to her awesome,
spring beauty

Eager Fields

As far as the eye can see,
the flat fields lie resting,
eerily quiet just now,
but ready and anxious
to get the season started.
They are quite ready
to prove their worth
producing bumper crops
and quite eager to show
just what they can do,
if only
their owners and tenants
continue to resist
the show of money
from the feared housing
and development industry

The Fragile Infant

There is but little life left
within her frail body,
so how is she to continue
giving life
to the restless, waiting,
innocent, crying lips
of the fragile infant
cradled in her arms?
Fighting back tears
that now scarcely come,
she wonders where she,
or they,
or we,
or He,
or who,
went wrong,
but finds no answer
worthy of scrutiny
as she begins
another feeding

Love Is Hope

Love is not
the answer to everything;
sometimes,
it merely gives us
the hope
that we desperately need
to help
in validating the good
and mitigating the bad,
with the eternal optimism
that the good
will always prevail

Tired Eyes Without Glow

Her eyes are very tired,
showing years and years
of accumulated hardships.
The glow that used to keep
the liveliness awake
has all but disappeared,
and her time
appears to be running out.
There is nothing now
that I can do
to bring back the glow,
so I just gently smile
my love to her,
and hold her hand
every chance I get.
I only hope
that she feels my love,
and that it is soothing
to her worn-out body

Letting Go Of The Precious

The depth of my sorrow
in parting
with a piece of my valley
is somewhat like
that which we feel as parents
when our children leave home
in pursuit of their dreams.
At best, it is difficult to accept,
but it is also obvious to us
that even strangers
must share a role
in shaping their delicate destiny.
Like parents with undecided hearts
who are yet to feel comfortable
letting go of their children,
such is my view
on parting with some of my hills,
which will always remain precious
in my bruised, hurting heart

Fresh, Time-Tested Love

Like happiness arriving
with the warm, quiet,
spring sunrise
when one anticipates a day
with their newly found love,
such is my happiness today
when I hold her hand.
Even though our love
is seasoned
and time-tested,
it remains as fresh
as it was in the beginning
when it was the one
that was newly found

Calloused Hands And Old Times

Many years ago,
a man's honesty
could be quickly assessed
by observing
his calloused hands
and weathered brow,
but times have changed.
Now, hands are
seldom calloused;
thus, we must find
new ways
of assessing one's honesty.
Suffice it to say,
I miss
those calloused hands
and old times,
and what they brought
with them

Loving Her Is So Easy

Loving her is so easy
that I completely forgot
about the past sting
of love gone bad,
and hopefully,
if she continues to show
her natural loveliness,
and I continue
to recognize it,
I will never have to focus
on the issue
of failed love again

Replenishing Depreciated Love

It may be unwise to assume
that the love
one shares today
will last forever.
Indeed, love seems to
naturally depreciate daily,
and it must be
replenished daily,
lest it runs out
before any realizes
that it has even diminished

Snowflakes Invasion

The large, aggressive
snowflakes
begin their fast, furious
descent upon us,
as if to implement
an invasion by surprise,
but the warm ground
hardly flinches,
obliterating them
as fast as they come,
without even
firing a shot

A Snail's Attitude

With the comforts of home
upon her back,
the snail crawls along
slowly and contentedly,
and because it matters little
how far she travels,
she carries no worries
with her.
Whatever today
or tomorrow brings,
she can either face it directly,
or she can simply
withdraw into her room
and quietly ignore it
if the mood so hits her.
Furthermore, she can stay in
or come out
whenever she feels like it,
without consequences
as we know them.
A snail's attitude is not so bad

Feeding With Love

Remembering the fish
and loaves of bread
that fed thousands,
one should freely
spread their love
all about,
then sit back
and watch it grow,
having ample faith
that it will feed
all of those
who have a want,
need,
and hunger for it

Sound Of The Dinner Bell

I can still remember
the sound of the dinner bell
as Mama rang it
to call us in from our distant work
away from the house.
We welcomed the sound,
not only for the anticipation
of her hot, home-cooked meal,
but also for the break that it gave us
from our tiring labor in the fields.
There was usually no need
to ring the bell in the evening,
because dusk would normally indicate
that it was time for supper.
Again, we would put aside our fatigue
at the busy table
long enough to enjoy
another hot, home-cooked meal
as we shared the day's highlights
with each other.
We would somehow find time
for inside or outside play
to complement our weary day.
Lastly, we would welcome sleep
to replenish our depleted bodies,
in preparation for doing it
all over again the next day,
when we would again
patiently anticipate the welcomed
sound of the dinner bell

Principles Of Work And Laziness

The children in our family
had little choice
when it came to choosing
work or laziness.
Our father believed
that laziness generated laziness,
and since he was not lazy,
he did not tolerate laziness
in his own family.
After we became adults
and had ample years
to think over his principles,
we became more understanding
of his seemingly harsh decisions.
Because he held steadfast
to his principles
of work and laziness,
we acquired part of his wisdom,
and it was much easier for us
to justify imparting
some of that same wise advice
to our own children

Participating In The Day

The day
suddenly changed
from mundane
to appealing,
catering just to me,
all because I decided
to participate in it,
rather than merely
choosing to sit back
and observe it
from a safe distance

A Divided, Richer Life

One's life is cut into half
when they make the choice
to walk with another,
and it is further divided
with the birth
of each subsequent child.
That is not reason to fret,
but rather rejoice,
because their life then
has potential
to be much, much richer
when shared
with their loved ones,
unless of course,
they selfishly decide
to keep too much of it
unto themselves

Softness In Her Eyes

Her big brown eyes
are much harder to read
than I anticipated,
but I believe
that softness is in there
just the same.
It is just waiting
to be shared
with someone showing
sufficient time,
love, and patience
to truly read it

The Awkward Dinner

The farmer sits at the table
with his wife of fifty years,
making small talk with her
to keep from thinking about
what others at the long table
must be saying about them.
They are here
only because their son believes
that their pleasures
should be expanded,
but they both know
that they do not belong here
among those who are obviously
above associating with them.
Little do the others know
that he would not trade places
with any of them,
nor would he trade
bank accounts,
even when he lightheartedly
knows that doing so
would undoubtedly favor him.
He pauses his dinner
as he reaches under the table
to take her hand,
and she smiles softly
at his welcomed gesture,
because they both know
that their pleasures here
are temporarily suppressed

Those Of Influence

I have a mind
of my own.
I do not want,
nor do I need,
those of influence
telling me
what to do,
what to say,
and how to think.
Ownership of fortune,
whether by privilege
or merit,
does not in itself
make anyone
wiser than another,
but it does
tend to make them
more complacent,
self-righteous,
and self-serving,
none of which
those with proper mind
need to have shared
with them

Pressing On Harder And Higher

I can only hope
that He is watching her
and listening to her,
and that He will give her
more time,
more precious time.
She needs more time
to do all the things
that we get to do,
but take for granted,
like living and breathing,
like loving a spouse,
like raising a child,
like pursuing dreams,
like loving family,
like having opportunity
to grow old naturally,
all without pain.
I also hope
that she presses on
harder and higher
and always has faith
that the miracle
lies just ahead

Minding Our Own Business

The cattle speckle the valley's hillsides,
lazily grazing about
minding their own business,
oblivious to unknowns around them
that are of no concern.
If only they knew how lucky they were,
they would most likely raise their tails
and race down the hills in pure delight.
After watching the evening news,
I would just like to
make myself oblivious to the world,
and simply admire
the cattle speckling the valley's hillsides
while they and I alike go about
minding our own business

What A Wonderful World It Could Be

What a wonderful world
it could be,
if rights and wrongs
were connected
to immediate cause-and-effect.
If appropriate rewards
immediately followed the rights,
all would learn the treasures
fast and well,
and hunger for more,
and eventually perpetuate
the beauty of rights to others.
If appropriate punishment
immediately followed the wrongs,
all would learn the perils
fast and well,
and try to further avoid them,
and eventually perpetuate
the severity of wrongs to others.
The good at heart
would feel wonderful
embracing the right way,
while the bad at heart
would fear the wrong way,
maybe enough
to begin embracing the right way.
What a wonderful world
it could be

The Barn Of Hard Play
And Fond Memories

The barn used to be so happy
when she hosted
and welcomed
the neighborhood kids,
but she seldom smiles now
because no one comes
to play anymore;
she was repurposed,
and she now lives for business only.
Sure, she knows
that she did not develop any stars
or great competitors,
but everyone so enjoyed
the hard play
which developed
so many happy children
and heaps of fond memories.
She thinks about today's children,
those pressured to become adults
before their time,
and she wishes
that she could borrow their innocence
for just one day,
to show them
what hard play and fond memories
are all about

Worn-Out Pants

In my generation,
our jeans were called pants,
and before that,
they were called britches.
They came from the factory
in pristine condition,
without any holes and tears.
Holes and tears
would come later
from hard work and hard play,
not because
of their styling appeal.
Moreover, had we known
that our worn-out pants
would develop
such a lucrative market,
we would have saved them all
for future gain

Early Rising Moon

The moon rises
extremely early,
even before her adversary
finishes his day,
but she quietly blends in
for a while
without being noticed,
save by those,
who, like me,
are so deeply in love
with beauty
that they notice such things
without being prompted

The Depth Of Our Love

While many would define love
as directly proportional
to the size of the stone
upon her finger,
she would define it
as the way I look into her eyes,
or the way
that I hold her hand
with predictable regularity.
That is fine with the both of us,
knowing that each of us
understands
and fully appreciates
the real depth
of the other's love

The Forgotten Snowman

For a while, the snowman
was nearly beside himself
with brazen joy
over the happiness
that the children displayed
in building him.
However, now that
the children have gone
to other interests,
and he is nearly spent,
he feels sadness
and a hint of jealousy
in being abandoned.
Moping and feeling sorry
for himself,
he anticipates
that it will be difficult
to get through
his last days alone,
not so much unlike
that felt by the elderly
when they feel forgotten
during their waning years

My Greatest Fear Conquered

I have already conquered
my greatest fear in life,
that of not being needed
and wholly loved by another;
additionally, because my cup
has been so generously filled
with so much abiding love,
I am no longer afraid
of passing with emptiness,
together with her,
or alone without her

Giving Away Love

Some believe
that giving away love
would eventually result
in its absolute depletion.
I believe
that giving away love
only activates
and stimulates it,
allowing it to prosper
and multiply exponentially.
The end result
of the latter theory
is that we could have
an infinite supply of love,
surely able to encompass
all that could ever be
wanted, needed, used,
or given away
in our lifetime

Love To The Moon And Back

I must admit
that I was wrong in saying
that my love for her
was equal to that of
'to the moon and back.'
It just dawned on me
that the distance
to the moon
is essentially quantified,
and that will never change,
whereas my perpetual
love for her
is constantly increasing.
I therefore rescind
my thoughtless analogy
because it implied
that my love for her
would never grow.
In reality,
I am fortunate to find it
infinitely unrestricted

The Four-Leaf Clover

I am so lucky to have found
that four-leaf clover
when I was a child.
It paved my way for
growing up in the country,
having a great childhood,
becoming friends with nature,
getting a good education,
settling into a nice vocation,
becoming a competitive runner,
having a wonderful daughter,
owning the land that I loved,
being blessed with good health,
becoming a passionate writer,
finding the love of my life,
having wonderful grandchildren,
and being happy.
Whew!
There was certainly a lot riding
on finding that four-leaf clover

Collective, Sad Moods

The quiet, colored sun
slowly and sadly walks away
until he disappears,
despondent over having
to leave us
with the gloom of darkness
until tomorrow.
As I continue reflecting
on she who continues
to valiantly fight
her losing bout with cancer,
I surmise
that I may have misperceived
the sun's sad mood,
as well as the sad mood
of everything about me;
maybe, I am just shouldering
the sadness of that
which we cannot control

The Time Warp

It seems only yesterday
that I shyly gave her
the fragrant array of roses
upon our first meeting.
Such has been the time warp
for nearly two decades
since our separate hearts
began singing together,
and since we began
unconsciously measuring
time and happiness
solely by moments
spent together

Gathering The Wood Chips

My family saw our father swing his double-bitted axe
for hours on end in the cold winter temperatures,
chopping logs into chunks waiting to be devoured by
our wood-guzzling heating stove common to the era.
His day of chopping would leave behind a large pile
of wood chips, and as the youngest child,
it was my job to gather those for fire-starting,
as well as helping my siblings carry the wood inside.
The more-pleasant warmer seasons
were too precious to be wasted on wood-gathering,
those months having been relegated
to putting aside food for our large family
and raising crops for our livestock's winter survival.
Decisions like that were a heavy load for our father,
and as harsh as we believed him to be,
I now surmise that he was wise beyond his years.
We worked hard, but we played even harder,
and it was evident to me that our father found ways
to cleverly sneak in allotted play time for us
without exposing any sign of parent weakness.
The resulting memories from our rationed play
tend to override our dismay felt with too much work.
I would be skeptical reliving some of my childhood,
but I somewhat miss gathering the wood chips,
going out into the pasture to bring in the milk cows,
and playing exciting bouts of tag and hide-and-seek.
If our father were still here,
I could easily visualize him chopping wood
with that same axe that he used most of his life,
and creating flying wood chips for me to gather

Using Our Love Wisely

Even though the love
in our home
was divided
among eleven children,
there was ample
for everyone,
but after the each of us
had received our share,
it was up to us individually
to use it wisely,
cuddle it,
and protect it,
so that it would grow
and multiply,
and serve us well
the entirety of our lives

The Blacktopped Road

When the gravel country road
that ran by our house
was blacktopped,
the children in my family rejoiced.
We thought that our simple world
had just gotten so much better.
Our bicycle-riding and tire-rolling
would be greatly improved,
but we had not given thought
to it bringing about
the end of our slingshot era.
With the gravel road,
we could gather
a convenient pocketful
of round shooting rocks
in only a matter of minutes,
and those would last us all day.
The blacktopped road
changed all that,
because it effectively took away
one of our favorite pastimes

Tiny Violets In The Wood

Because of their inherent,
shy nature,
the tiny violets
blend cleverly
into the large wood,
but I have trained myself
to diligently seek them out.
They help appease
my constant, selfish desire
to bring beauty
and value to my day,
but I hopefully reciprocate
by contributing
to their restrained,
timid hunger
for recognition as well

Pocketed Troubles

A day in the wood
is neither wasted, nor lost,
but rather well-spent,
when one realizes
and accepts
that their troubles will be
intuitively pocketed
for a short rest while there

Love's Rainy Days

Although love will have
some gloomy, rainy days,
a little rain
never hurts anyone;
on the contrary,
it should provoke
prudent thought
and appreciation of love,
while combating
ever reckless
complacency

Sorrow And Faith

Sorrow-filled days
will eventually pass
without soul-altering
consequence,
should one learn
to categorize sorrow
where it rightly belongs,
as the exception,
and categorize faith
where it rightly belongs,
as the rule

Bettering The Days Of Friends

If one will only
open the door,
a friend will come in
and sit with them
through their story,
whether it is
a handsome story
or an ugly story.
By the story's end,
it will have
bettered the days of both,
the talker
for having found a friend
unafraid to listen,
and the listener
for having found a friend
unafraid to talk

The Heart's Capacity

The heart has
only so much space
within it;
therefore, be sure
to fill it with love
to near-capacity,
thereby allowing
less room
for undesirable traits
to take root and grow

Ms. Nature's Approval

The opinions are many
and varied
regarding Ms. Nature's
approval of us.
My guess
is that she loves us most
when we have spent
quality time with her,
but have taken away
nothing except
nice memories, respect,
and admiration for her,
leaving everything
undisturbed
and ready
for the next visitor
to enjoy

The Country Summer Night

The country summer night
comes in softly and quietly,
accompanied only
by the sounds
of Ms. Nature's children
telling each other
of their happiness.
That is reason enough
to let her sleep peacefully,
as I give silent thanks
for the opportunity
to reside in Heaven on Earth,
that is, in the calm,
blissful country

Life Partner

We go to bed
together
every night,
warmly embracing
each other
until sleep comes,
and I am unsure
that I could even
sleep without her,
Ms. Nature,
my life partner

My Long Run Elation

The misty drizzle
begins so gently
that I can hardly tell
it is lightly caressing
my bare arms.
Because it brings
such welcomed elation
with it on this warm
summer evening,
I smile to myself
and pick up the pace
with lighter feet
and more eager heart,
as I turn to head home
on my daily, long run

Living My Story

My story is most likely
interesting only to me,
and it is most likely
monotonous to others,
much like the story
that all of us portray.
If I were to
live my story differently,
against my will,
I would suppose
that my enthusiasm
would greatly suffer,
and my story
would then
not only be drab
to others,
but also drab to me

The Mysterious Fog

The fog creeps into the valley
like a mysterious stranger,
unsure of what to do
and where to go
at this late hour.
Finally, he stows himself away
in the infinite darkness
to quietly develop a plan
for the rest of tonight
and tomorrow morning

The Hibernating Brook

The country brook awakens
from her long hibernation
to greet the warm, gentle day.
After several hours
bathing her body
and rejuvenating her soul
in the fresh spring air,
she begins to play
and run about
with her spirited friends
as they robustly embrace
the new season

Sour Apple Memories

Long ago,
the sour apple tree
deceivingly lured
me and my siblings
away from work and play.
Even as our parents
articulated its logical
drawbacks to us,
we still always placed
more importance
on instant gratification
over ensuing bellyaches.
We may have even shown
a hint of wisdom,
since the memories
of the sour apples
remain with us,
while the bellyaches lasted
only a short while

My Memory-Collecting

Of all the memories
that I have collected
during my life,
my years on Pipe Creek
are the ones
that have been my fondest
and weathered
the test of time.
I do not mean to imply
that my years there
were my easiest;
on the contrary,
they were among
my hardest.
However, they seemed
to always be carefree hard,
and they were intermittently
mixed with carefree play.
My memories there
have been impossible to top,
and that has made
all the difference
in my memory-collecting

The Financially-Exclusive

It is the gruesome way
of the financially-exclusive
to make certain
that the common
not only pay their own bills,
but also pay an unfair chunk
of the financially-exclusive's
bills as well.
Such is the shame
of our good and bad,
capitalistic system
when ridden with loopholes
that are designed or lobbied
by those same,
financially-exclusive
who benefit from them

The Sly Groundhog

The sly groundhog slowly emerges
from his warm bed,
wipes the sleep from his eyes,
and sticks his toes out the door
to test the weather.
Not impressed by what he feels,
he makes up this cockamamie story
about seeing his shadow,
saying that he is unable
to come out for another six weeks
because winter is still not done.
All of this appears to be
mere justification for craving
an additional six weeks
of idleness and sleep
to pamper his plump body,
thereby escaping whatever work
groundhogs are obligated to do.
Some even believe his flimsy story,
which matters little to him,
because he will be sleeping regardless

The Cozy Cabin

The cozy cabin
at the edge of the woods
looks like he belongs there
and wants to be there,
and he even seems
to be unconcerned
about how
the distant neighbors
might feel about him.
The road to the cabin
is little more than a trail,
and that seems to be
the way he likes it as well.
He appears calm
and so much at home there,
where things are quiet
and serene,
where the day
is all about relaxation,
and where life is quite livable,
without unnecessary,
unwanted interruptions

Counting Days And Evenings

I have no time to count
the days and evenings
that I have yet to spend
among the hills in the valley,
because I have been
too busy enjoying
the days and evenings
already spent there,
that being a full-time,
enjoyable matter for those
well learned in enjoying

On Love Waiting

Love will wait on one
only so long,
and after that,
it will move along
to be with anyone
who will recognize it,
appreciate it,
and treat it
with the respect
it justly deserves

Telling Esther Of Her Loveliness

Although she obviously
could not find enough things
to be grateful for
at that given time,
surely there could have been
sufficient purpose in her life
to orchestrate forgiveness
for her mistake.
Times were different then,
and mistakes were not meant
to be confronted
and talked through,
but rather, concealed
from a judging public.
I, and plenty others,
could have told Esther
of her loveliness,
and that her mistake
would not
forever define her life,
had she only given us
the chance
before she took her own life

What Would Or Could Have Been

It is scary to think about what would have been,
had not my high school friend convinced me
to make an intuitive change to my life vocation,
had not the Vietnam War been a current issue,
had not my military ambitions been reversed by fate,
had not my college direction stayed on course
after temporary diversion by military objectives,
had not my future employer visited my college
for interviews that resulted in a job offering for me,
had not I turned down two other job offers before
accepting that job where I would work most of my life,
had not I taken vacation from my job that August week,
had not I agreed to work with my siblings
on a construction project that same vacation week,
had not it rained that day to postpone our work,
had not I utilized that day off for a leisurely drive,
had not I met her while driving around that day,
had not we had our first date that evening,
had not we continued seeing each other regularly,
had not we gotten married,
had not we been blessed with a daughter,
had not we gotten a divorce after twenty years,
had not I allotted myself five years to become
reacquainted with myself and find my direction,
had not I met another woman with ultimate loveliness,
and had not we stayed together to complete
each other's life for a splendid second chance.
Indeed, it is scary to think about what would have been,
or could have been,
with even one slight deviation along the way

Occupants Of Home

My heart wants to go home again,
but I know that is not possible;
sure, the house stands there still,
but the occupants have changed
since it was my home.
All that I can do now
is reach deeply within my soul
and try to remember
my old home as best I can,
try to retrieve and remember
the good times made there,
and try to remind others
to go home more often,
while their old home occupants
live there still,
while it yet qualifies as home

Front Porches

Front porches are nice to look at,
but they are of little value anymore
except to those who have
nothing better to do
than watch others go by.
Back when people
frequently called upon
family and neighbors,
porches were used for visiting
and evening relaxation.
Then, they were still adorned
with well-worn rocking chairs
that were used
to help celebrate the day's blessings,
rock away their day's troubles,
and help them rest long enough
to think about
tomorrow's blessings or hiccups

Earned Through Effort

In my youth, trophies and awards
were given because they were earned,
not just because one participated,
and sparing hurt feelings
for not having gotten one
was not a high priority.
Such treatment was our introduction
to the real world early on.
We had little need for high-fives
or being told that we were great
when we knew
that we were not great.
That is not to say
that those who did not get awards
were simply losers,
any more than it is to say
that those who did get awards
were simply winners,
but it is to say that those
who did get awards earned them,
the hard way,
the honest way,
through hard effort,
not just through participation

Generational Knowledge

If one would find humor
with those before us
who believed that the world was flat,
then they should also recognize
that those following us
may sneer at our knowledge
and likewise judge us
with that same humor.
Knowledge is only relative
to our respective generation,
which is why those behind us
will judge us
by the knowledge of their generation,
thereby making the same unfair
repetitive judgments.
It is about much more
than just being aware
of old knowledge
and old ways.
Each generation is obligated
to raise the bar
by discovering and creating knowledge
that will pave the way anew
and challenge the next generation
to do even more

Riding Down Saplings

I hope Ms. Nature
will forgive me and my siblings
for riding down
some of her young,
innocent saplings in the wood.
That was one
of our favorite means of play
back in our day,
but we gave little thought
to the damage
that we might be leaving behind.
Even though
the stronger saplings
surely were hardly affected,
some of the weaker ones
certainly may have never
stood upright again.
We were just fortunate
that our father
failed to ever catch us
participating in this damaging,
potentially-dangerous mischief

His Friend, The Pocketknife

My father's pocketknife
went everywhere
that he went;
if it could not go somewhere,
then he did not need
to go there either.
It was his good friend,
and even though
he often habitually
subjected it to abuse
by using it many ways
for which it was not intended,
he would carefully
swipe the blades
across his britches leg
to clean them
before putting the knife
back into his pocket,
like anyone would do
who cared
for such a good friend

Two Purple Violets

On this unusually warm,
early-March day,
two tiny purple violets
show themselves to the world,
and I, having long been
a lover of wild violets
in the wood,
do not let them go unnoticed.
I take a moment to squat
and greet them,
and I welcome them
to another fine, promising spring
before moving on
to look for other wild violets
to welcome

Old Wash Pans

Today's ornate, elegant
faucets and sinks
have replaced
the old porcelain
and galvanized wash pans
that sat alongside
community bars
of Lava hand soap
and messy soap dishes.
It is just as well
because few soil their hands
enough anymore
to mandate the use of Lava.
I still miss the old wash pans,
and even though
they were impractical
and unsanitary,
I miss them because
they remind me
of the simpler days
that will never return again

Love Is The Best That We Have

Love may not be
the answer to everything,
but it is
a mighty handsome start.
Since hate and conflict
are not feasible options,
it looks like love
is about the best
that we have available.
So, we should get used to it,
learn to use it,
learn to embrace it,
and definitely
learn to perfect the use of it

The Butterfly Garden

After I spent great effort
building the garden
of wildflowers,
the many varieties
of beautiful butterflies
began arriving
with increasing numbers.
It became second nature for me
to just sit and watch them
while they ran about
as young children without worries,
heedless of time and promises.
Their happiness with garden play,
and my happiness watching them,
taught me to rearrange
my priorities
and save more of my work
for the uncertain tomorrows,
while allowing more beauty
to permeate my certain todays

Age Of My Will And Way

I find myself wondering
how age quietly crept up on me;
it is as though
I have never turned around
to see where I have been,
and yet, I know that I have.
My will
rivals that of youngsters,
but my way
clearly speaks of significant years
beyond my will,
so I just think
that I will let this matter of age
lie to rest for a while longer,
as peaceably as I can,
until my will and way
are separated by fewer years,
and I may then reevaluate each
to see how I feel about aging

Newness Of Spring

The first weeks of spring
are a wonderful time.
The newness
and excitement
of the coming season
clean our slate
of winter problems
and remind us
that our winter worries
were likely less severe
than first believed.
It is an opportune time
to replace
old, winter memories
with new, spring memories
while the newness of spring
yet has our attention

Time Nearly Used Up

If the time should arrive
when I am hesitant
about being glad
to be alive
in the day which is born
with natural splendor,
then I think it is surely time
to begin thinking
about giving up my fight.
It may be time
to turn over my problems
to another
with adequate spunk
and enthusiasm
to confront them
more efficiently than I,
which is to say,
it may be time to admit
that I am merely a shell
of my former self,
and my useful time
is nearly used up

The Haves And Have-Nots

I could easily be sympathetic
with the have-nots,
did I not remember
the many years
that I constructively spent
overcoming
my own hardships,
all the while
establishing my own set
of enduring work ethics.
As I remember
those hard years now,
and I realize
that I was strengthened,
not weakened by them,
I am motivated to motivate
the have-nots.
I encourage them
to get off their bottoms
and establish their own set
of stringent work
and worth ethics,
which will naturally
help them migrate smoothly
from the have-nots
to the haves

Squandering Autumn Days

After enduring
month after month
of winter's misery,
it is quite easy to embrace
the welcoming April sunshine
and forget
that we barely made it
through another winter.
One would rationally reason
that our accumulated
age and wisdom
would better prepare us
for subsequent winters,
but it hardly seems
to ever work that way.
Thus, we will
probably continue
squandering autumn days
until the winter, yet again,
unexpectedly slaps us
squarely in the face

Love, *A Gift Or Detriment*

Only you can decide
whether your love
is a gift or a detriment.
I could decide for you,
but I doubt
that we would agree
because my answer is biased.
Give it some honest thought,
and perhaps your answer
may even surprise yourself;
meanwhile, I will be here,
if you need any subtle advice,
howbeit slightly biased

Game Of Following The Green

No one knows
just when Ms. Nature
has accumulated
enough glorious green
to declare spring
fully upon us,
only that she knows.
This game,
this shrewd game
of following the green
that keeps us guessing
and hoping,
is well worth everyone's
fullhearted participation

That Small Gesture

When I first gathered
nerve enough
to simply hold her hand,
my reaction
was an automatic response
that momentarily
took my breath away.
Although we have come far
since that magical moment,
I still take great delight
in holding her hand,
that same small gesture
which initially won me over,
and that same small gesture
which continues to enrich
our lasting relationship

Rectifying Regrets Together

I apologize for all that I missed,
for missing her first kiss,
for missing her first date,
for missing her prom,
for missing her high school graduation,
for missing her going off to college,
for missing her marriage,
for missing the birth of her two sons,
for missing her divorce,
for missing the opportunity
of sharing a solid, happy life with her.
I missed all of that
simply because
it was before I even met her,
before I knew
that I was destined to meet her.
Now that I get to be with her,
I plan on not missing out
on anything else;
furthermore, I plan to make up
for all that I missed,
for all that she missed,
even as it should be
when two of destiny
are rectifying regrets together

My Second Life

I vividly remember
the suffering
at the end of my first life
when we parted ways.
It was a painful time,
laden with sorrow
and regret,
and though He chose
to give me a second life,
enthusiasm was not
easy to come by.
I had to ease into caring
about anything,
and anyone,
but I somehow held on
and gained the patience
that I sorely needed.
I was able to slowly heal,
and I learned to live again;
then, I met her,
and I learned to love again.
That is why I am so glad
that I decided
to give my second life
a fair chance

Learning From Children's Play

Some problems are rightly reserved
to be taken to the bench in the park;
there, one can pause their problems
and give their mind a rest
while watching the children play.
If they watch with their heart,
they may see
that the problems
which were really bothering them
may be less severe
than first perceived.
One can be neither too busy,
nor too smart,
to sit for a few quiet moments
at the nonjudging bench,
to relax,
to solve their problems,
to learn from the children
as they sit to watch them
laugh and play

Resolving Hardships

There is not much
that anyone can tell me
about common,
day-to-day hardships
that I do not know already.
I cannot say
that I have addressed
all my hardships
with adequate enthusiasm,
but addressed them I have,
even if only out of obligation.
I cannot even say
that I have resolved
all my hardships
with satisfactory resolutions,
but resolved them I have,
even if only to the best
of my meager ability.
If any does not
get the picture,
then I can only surmise
that someone has been
habitually following along
behind them for some time,
addressing and resolving
their hardships for them

How Can Someone Not Love Us?

One may be wondering
why everyone
does not have
a special someone
to love them,
and that is obviously
a valid concern.
Such mystery is not unlike
that perceived
by many others every day,
but someday,
sometime,
somewhere,
someone may unexpectedly
come along
to sweep them off their feet,
assuming that they are
willing to be swept.
At least that is something
all can hope for

Hands Not Touched For A While

I thought I saw
a glimpse
of lonely gentleness
in her eyes,
but I wanted to be sure
before I mistakenly
reached out
to touch her hands.
Even if that
is what I truly saw,
I need to understand
that she may be cautious
about someone touching
her lonely hands
that may not have been
touched for a while.
That is not
to be taken lightly,
because hands
not used to being touched
by one who cares
can instinctively withdraw,
even as they ache
to be touched.
This I know,
having once had hands
that had not touched,
and been touched,
for a while

Slowing Down For Each Other

Where are we going
in such haste?
Surely that which awaits
at our destination
is not so important
as the love beckoning
in our hearts.
We need to slow down
so that everyone
is permitted a few moments
to look into
each other's eyes and heart,
if for no other reason
than to satisfy our thoughts
about what could have been,
or what yet could be

The Mood Set By Spring

The warm, welcomed,
spring day
wonderfully sets the mood
for those longing to love
and to be loved,
making it so much easier
and authentic to smile,
even when unaware
of their smiling.
This mood
encourages those
with lonely, longing hearts
to silently flirt with those
having similar hearts,
all the while
hoping for a love miracle

Playing About With Hearts

It is not at all proper
for one to be a heartbreaker
just because they can be.
The heart is a delicate instrument
through which
all can color their world
bright or gloomy,
and anyone's heart
is just as meaningful as another's.
One should never assume
that it is fair game
to frivolously play about
with hearts,
but rather they should
treat each heart
as if it were at-risk
and meant to be shared
only with those of good intent

Glory And Character

It is not a shame
for one to live their life
without glory.
Glory is nice,
but it fades as easily
as the setting sun;
however, character
is a different matter.
It is a shame
for one to live their life
without character.
Character is that of which
the strong, honest,
and durable
are made,
and when one earns
sound character,
that will speak volumes
about the legacy it aids
in leaving behind

The Tall Oak Tree

Like a giant,
the tall oak tree
dwarfs those around him,
reaching toward the sky
as if to assert his sovereignty.
Those who know him best
know that his show
is nothing like
his normal demeanor.
They know
that he is not snubbing them,
but that he is really
just one of them,
except a bit more daring
in showing off his masculinity

Hand And Heart

Should giving me her hand
in exchange for my heart
happen with
the simple integrity
with which it is intended,
there should be
little else that matters
to either of us
the remainder of our life

Reaching To Give And Get

Our hearts
have an infinite capacity
for love,
and those who understand this
reach freely
to give and get
more love.
Unfortunately, there are
some who refuse
to acknowledge this,
getting sidetracked
with hate,
allowing it to grow,
and grow,
and grow,
until it can no longer
be contained.
Eventually,
when these troubled souls
reach to give and get,
there is only hate
within their range,
easily empowering
that irrepressible cycle of crime
that often follows

Time For Play

Although many may mislead us
into believing
that there will always be time
for play later,
it may be unwise
to delay our play too long.
Sure, work must come first,
at least for those willing
to pull their own weight,
but work must be
well-balanced with play.
Too little play
may yield a dull and grouchy manner,
while too much play
may foster irresponsibility and laziness;
therefore, play now,
play often,
play hard,
even play tired,
but play wisely.
There will certainly be time
for rest later,
and there will probably be time
for play later,
but our vigor may not always
match our will to support play then.
It is also unlikely
that play will be as enjoyable later,
so choose playtime wisely
for balanced gratification

A Lawn For My Nature Friends

A groomed lawn
is not welcoming
for my nature friends,
so I groom it lightly,
not to look good or great,
but rather to not look so badly.
Even though it means
endorsing dandelion heaven,
I would rather groom lightly
and see
all my nature friends
playing about,
than groom comprehensively
and see
none of my nature friends
playing about

The Power Of Spring

If anything can help him
forget about her
being gone,
it is surely
the power of spring.
When spring emerges,
everything is reborn
and springs to life
right before our very eyes.
Those without purpose
begin searching for purpose,
and those with declining will
begin wanting to live again,
or so it seems anyway,
when the power of spring
begins working its charm

Fun At A Cost Of Nothing

Having fun was more fun,
and cheaper, in my youth.
I could contemplate fantasy for hours
while lying on the creekbank
with crossed legs
and a stem of timothy in my lips,
at a cost of nothing;
I could roll an old automobile tire
on the country road for miles
before I tired,
at a cost of nothing;
I could arm myself against predators
with a homemade slingshot
and pockets bulging with ammo rocks,
at a cost of nothing;
I could catch fireflies after dark
and watch them glow in a jar
with a lid full of holes,
at a cost of nothing.
I could swim in our summer creek
and catch tadpoles and crawdads
until darkness called me home,
at a cost of nothing.
Yes, I am quite certain
I have supported my belief
that having fun was more fun,
and cheaper, in my youth,
than in my adulthood

Just To Know What It Is Like

Everyone should experience hunger
for a few days,
just to know what it is like,
and to gain appreciation for having
an abundance of food.
Everyone should sleep in the elements
for a few nights,
just to know what it is like,
and to gain appreciation for having
comfortable shelter.
Everyone should be impoverished
for a few days,
just to know what it is like,
and to gain appreciation for having
adequate finances.
Everyone should dress in rags
for a few days,
just to know what it is like,
and to gain appreciation for having
stylish clothing.
Everyone should live with nature
for a few days,
just to know what it is like,
and to gain appreciation for sharing
her abundant beauty.
Everyone should be without love
for a few days,
just to know what it is like,
and to gain appreciation for having
that which keeps the world turning

The Strong Survive And Provide

Knowing that the stronger
have survived better
for century after century
should alone be
enough motivation
for everyone
to toughen themselves,
beginning at the age
of accountability.
However, exposure
to easier living
has substantially softened
the masses,
so that now
it is quite common
for many to naturally choose
the path of least resistance.
That is fine until they are tested,
at which time the stronger
are usually required to provide
for the weaker,
without any due accountability
required of the latter

Frolicking Calves And Children

The young calves frolic about
in the spring-greened pasture,
inventing their play as they go,
free of all worry and care
so long as their keepers
and providers
are within safe distance,
which is the way
it was meant to be,
whether it is young calves
in pastures and meadows,
or our own children
in yards, parks, and meadows

Right Things In Our Home

I cannot imagine
that there was much reason to rejoice
when I was born,
because I was the last of eleven children;
moreover, it would mean
that my father and mother had to produce
even more food than before
for the busy table.
Looking back, the right things in our home
must have well exceeded the wrong things,
because good childhood memories
seem to be prevalent
with most of my siblings.
Although the love in our home
seemed to be mostly hidden,
it was embedded there just the same,
in quantity and quality enough
that it produced and nurtured
unmistakably happy children.
I have tried to be objective
in searching for faults in our home
that would justify disliking our youth,
but I cannot identify
any of consequence;
therefore, I must conclude
that we received a good and decent start,
and accountability
for all our adult actions
must be directed right back to ourselves,
where it rightfully belongs

Feeling Better When Down

When down, one can
easily make themselves
feel better
by listening to good 'ole
time-tested, upbeat,
gospel music.
If that does not
make them feel better,
they may need
to stop multi-tasking
and just get into the music.
If that does not
make them feel better,
then maybe their priorities
are misdirected
and only need to be realigned.
If that does not
make them feel better,
then they probably
do not want to feel better

Everyone Is Something

No one is nothing,
because everyone
is something,
so the responsibility
for any true,
significant deviation
from either
rests squarely
on the shoulders
of themselves,
and only themselves

Love Delivered

My professed love for her
has been signed, sealed,
and delivered to her,
so it is now
solely dependent upon her
to either open it
and decide
what she wants to do
with my love,
or not open it,
which is essentially
rejecting me.
I cannot even be objective
during this uncertain time,
and without a daisy to pluck,
I must merely await a reply,
which may or may not come,
to determine
whether she loves me
or loves me not

The Purpose Of Mountains

The massive mountains
of stone or trees
are not meant to be
scaled or explored
unless doing so
leaves no trace
of having been there.
Rather, they are there
to soothe and comfort
our souls and senses
and to assure all
that they will
remain there,
unblemished,
for our descendants
endless generations
to come

Hints Of Raw Beauty

The blue-and-white,
miniscule wild violet
tries to hide
among the leftover
winter leaves
and new spring growth,
but I, having a sharp eye
for such hints of raw beauty,
saw her right away.
Her shyness is safe with me,
because I only want
to admire her for a moment;
then, I will be moving on,
keeping my eye out
for other spring attractions
and similar hints
of raw beauty

Mischief-Makers

If one must participate
in damaging mischief
to pass the time,
they should become
well-acquainted
with community service
as acceptable restitution.
Those who lose possessions
born of toil
do not part with them lightly,
and they have little tolerance
for mischief
born of those
unfamiliar with toil.
That is not the way it is,
but that is the way
it should be,
known or unbeknown
to the mischief-makers

Discarding Shoes

Several generations ago,
a pair of shoes was a luxury,
worn part-time or not at all
during the summer,
their wear reserved
for the more-challenging winter.
Back then, shoes were prized
and well cared for,
and they were often refurbished
with new soles and laces as needed.
If they were outgrown,
they were never discarded,
but rather passed down
to a sibling or neighbor,
and so long as they were functional,
they were gladly accepted
and treated with utmost respect.
Now, shoes are worn mostly for style,
frequently retired prematurely
to a congested closet with friends,
where they lie unworn
for months or years.
They are eventually sorted,
still in good condition,
for final destination
at charitable organizations
or the waiting landfill,
quite a disappointment
considering the excitement
with which they were purchased

Beloved Or Hated Dirt

Dirt was once our friend
and companion;
it was worn as a badge of honor
because it indicated
that we had played hard,
without reserve,
and left nothing on the field.
The dirt was worn as long as possible,
until the bosses declared
that time had arrived for it to go.
In all seasons except winter,
my siblings and I accomplished this
by conveniently skinny-dipping
in our country creek.
Dirt has since become public enemy,
and it immediately alarms the bosses,
which inevitably leads
to hasty eradication
in the always-convenient shower.
Right, wrong, or indifferent,
that is one reason
why children find it difficult
to be children anymore

Love From Children And Dogs

Young children and dogs
will love you
when no one else will,
including yourself.
Yet they want
for nothing in return
except love
and a little attention,
if you can spare it,
so loving children and dogs
is obviously a win-win
for all concerned,
and it may even embellish
your love for yourself

Looking For Love

Looking for love
can sometimes seem
like an exhausting,
futile effort.
However, any search
requires a reasonable
tolerance for patience,
so one should never
give up hope.
A cautious readiness
should be maintained
at all times
so that,
at any moment,
they can begin
a new beginning
with that someone
who is equally eager
to share their life
with another

The Velvet Violet

The timid, velvet violet
just sits there quietly,
smiling without smiling,
unaware that she has
attracted attention
from an avid admirer,
and I,
realizing that her loveliness
is even greater
when she is not posing,
see no reason
to let her know differently

Pot-Bellied Wood Stoves

I well remember
that up close and friendly feeling
that came from
the pot-bellied wood stove.
It was so comfortable
that it made one temporarily forget
any troubles following them around.
I also well remember
that dreaded and unfriendly feeling
that came from
the same pot-bellied stove
after it had time
to guzzle its contents
and begin quickly cooling off,
which made one resort back
to the same troubles
that they had temporarily forgotten

Family Quarrels

Family quarrels were put on hold
for a short while
each time our joined hands
formed the rectangle
around the kitchen table at supper.
However, children being children,
they were quickly renewed
after supper,
as we scattered to find,
and possibly share,
evening play.
That worked quite well
for our large family
because the hand-joining
always subdued the severity
of our quarrels
and kept our undetectable love
for each other
alive and well

Love For Toys

The toys that my siblings and I
were fortunate enough to have
were normally very prized,
because our own time and effort
had usually been utilized
in making them.
They were treated well
because they were few
and hard to come by,
and because they could not
be easily duplicated
with ones having personalities
just like them.
Our toys were meant
to be enjoyed and appreciated,
not broken from abuse
and pure boredom.
That is why my love for toys
has stayed with me my entire life,
whether the toys are
man toys, now,
whether they were
boy toys, then,
or whether they are
boy toys, now

Extra Lovable With Love

I sincerely hope
that love does not
run out on me,
because it has done
just that before.
I think that I have not
the emotional strength
and will
to deal with it again,
so I am trying to be
extra lovable with love
to prevent it
from happening,
even more so than before

He Was Loved And Appreciated

They say that he died young
because of his years of hard work,
but I knew the man well,
and I think that he died of worry.
He was not afraid of hard work,
but rather he welcomed it;
he took pride in outworking others,
remembering that his father
had always told him
that hard work was his strength.
I remember that he constantly worried
that he would fail
in feeding his large family
and raising them properly,
but after he had fed them well
and raised them properly,
he then worried that he would fail
in providing for his wife
who had loved him so devoutly
for so many years.
The reason that he died is unimportant.
Even though he died too young,
what does matter
is that he was deeply loved
and appreciated
by his wife and large family,
proving that his abbreviated life
was not at all in vain

Juicy, Wild Raspberries

I am going out
to the pasture thicket in the wood
in search of juicy, wild,
black raspberries
that have been fed and nurtured
by early-summer's, gentle rain
and warm sun.
This time,
contrary to my father's
well-intended orders
directed toward his children,
I vow to eat every last one that I find,
until my mind and stomach
have been fully pleased.
For the first time in my life,
I pledge to return
with empty containers
and picking bucket
entirely void of berries for canning

The Old Man On The Bench

I could see that the old man
on the bench
had a lot of living under his belt,
clearly evidenced
by his deep wrinkles
and tough, weathered skin.
I knew that he had seen things
that I probably never would see,
and true to my way,
I slowly approached the bench
with a subtle smile.
Uninvited,
I quietly introduced myself
as I firmly shook his hand
before sitting down beside him.
I paused for a moment
gathering comfort
to ask him how he was,
and prepared to spend
the rest of the day
listening to his stories
and gleaning his wisdom

The Daisy's Beauty

Even though
the daisy's beauty
does not necessarily
rival that of her peers,
it holds a special place
in my impressionable heart.
Ever since
she shyly picked a daisy
and gave it to me
at our first outing,
its beauty has taken on
a fresh new meaning
that I shall not easily forget

Invaders Of The Wasps

Wasps are quite harmless
when left alone to guard their nest,
but they can be a bundle of terror
when aroused or provoked.
Most invasions are innocent
and even unknown to the invaders
until it is too late,
and showing natural fear
of the wasps
only intensifies their aggressiveness.
Life would be so much safer
for all involved
if the wasps would only make
better choices for their nest site,
allowing innocent invaders
to invade the privacy
of others less offensive

Stormy Chaos

She seems to be
in a very foul mood today,
sending down angry clouds,
indiscriminate, harassing winds,
and driving rains
all about us,
creating a stormy chaos
that we have yet learned
to harness.
Maybe that is why she does it,
just to remind us
that she is still in control,
and that we need to be
a little more respectful of her
during calm, normal times

Measuring Oneself
With Themself

When one uses the performance
and deeds of others
to gauge their own works,
they are, indeed,
limiting their own efforts
and setting themself up
for inert progress or failure.
One should measure themself
with themself,
and themself only,
and set about showing others
that success is possible
when combining their passion
with extremely hard efforts

Things That Matter

Like a gentle June drizzle,
the night falls softly
on those who have properly
arranged their priorities,
letting them calmly enjoy
the blessings of a gentle day
as they remember
the things that matter.
Meanwhile, for the worriers
who have yet to learn
about arranging their priorities,
it lets them continue worrying
about things that do not matter

The Pear Tree

No one pays attention
to the pear tree
except in early spring
when she is
showing off her blossoms,
and in fading fall
when she is
busy perfecting
her luscious fruit.
Just the same,
she is there the entire year,
sleeping, resting,
or nurturing her crop,
and doing whatever else
pear trees do
when no one is
paying attention to them

The Infamous Sidewalk

The rock sidewalk leading up to
the front door of our old homeplace
was laid long before
my family lived there.
Were it not for the changing times,
it would have been
relatively maintenance-free,
but times were changing
with greater social awareness,
so the sidewalk became
high-maintenance.
Since lawnmowers and weed-eaters
were luxuries and still in their infancy,
it required many child-hours
of kneeling on the large flat rocks
to pull crabgrass from between them.
It was not even relative
to ask the grass-pullers
if we thought
the appearance of the finished product
was worth our efforts,
because I am quite certain
that we never completely finished
manicuring the sidewalk.
Evidently the crabgrass grew faster
than we were able to work
with our allotted time devoted to it,
because we were forever deterred
with our gloomy attitudes
by not being able to stay ahead of it

Catching My Breath

I walked to the top
of the steep hill
after finishing
the morning chores,
stopping
for a few moments
to catch my breath,
only to lose it again
when I looked out
over the calm valley
that was just beginning
to fill up
with spring colors.
I spent the next
several hours
making extra sure
I had caught my breath
as I quietly sat
immersed
in the valley's beauty

Here Comes The Rain

She must believe
that she is actually helping,
because here comes
the rain again.
It is too soon
after yesterday's cloudburst,
and she must surely know
that most of today's rain
will be wasted
in this horrendous downpour.
It should have been saved
for another time
when it was more needed,
but she should know by now
what she is doing,
having been at it
almost forever

Scolded By The Robin

I have no idea
what the robin is saying,
but I do know
that she is scolding me
and giving me what-for.
I now see that I have gotten
too close to her nest,
so I believe that I will
just move right along
and pretend
that I did not hear
her nasty threats,
and let things get back
to her normal,
so both of us will be happy

The Official Drink-Holder

When it was decided
that all of us would be going
to the entertainment theme park,
I just assumed
that I would be in for a long day,
since my excitement is normally
best generated with other interests.
It was just like her,
to reach down
into her seven-year-old heart of gold,
and designate me
the official drink-holder.
Because she understood
that their exhilaration
was not my exhilaration,
she wanted to assure me
that I would not be left behind
and excluded from their day of fun,
but rather be needed
and ever present
to share in their excitement

The Big Spring

My siblings and I
always had a good time
at the Big Spring
during the long summers of our youth.
From bent knees and extended palms,
we assumed prone position
and drank often
from its clear, pure water
which had been filtered
through the ground
only seconds before,
and we sat on its shaded ledge to rest
while taking a short break
from our work in the hot fields.
Individually, we used its quietness
to sort out our petty problems of youth
and dream silent dreams
of the opposite gender
that we had a crush on.
It was a quiet, peaceful, well-used place,
unlike today,
when it remains dismally quiet
with neglect and abandonment
after the family's youth
matured and moved on

Country Air Pureness

All should take advantage
of every opportunity
to enjoy the freshness
of wooded country air,
because its present level
of pureness
will likely
never be matched again

Have A Heart

Have a heart,
and do not break my heart.
It has been broken before,
and I can attest to the fact
that it is quite painful
and nearly intolerable;
so, have a heart,
and let our hearts beat
softly and gently together,
without any fear
of losing synchronization

Our Legend

We are almost always
a legend to ourselves,
in our own mind,
in our own time,
but we are almost never
a legend to others,
in their own mind,
in their own time.
Either way,
it hardly matters,
because life goes on
quite well
with or without us,
and with or without
the legend
that stands beside us,
or the legend
that we hope follows us

Dream Versus Reality

Do not dream of another
too long,
but rather just long enough
for gaining ample nerve
to approach them.
Whether they react
with a sneer
or gentle smile,
you will have
followed your heart,
and the rest is up to them.
It may well be
the end
before it even began,
or it could be
the beginning
of love without end,
but nevertheless,
it will have become reality
as opposed
to only a dream

The Rose Stem

I leaned on the footbridge railing,
holding the red rose
that she had given me
shortly after we met many years ago.
Its present, dried-out life
was only a remnant of its former glory,
much like our love for each other.
One by one,
I plucked the fragile petals
and let them drop
into the unhurried water below,
until only the stem remained,
further reminding me
of our own stripped-down love.
There was nothing left worth saving
of the rose or our love,
so I pitched the stem into the water
and quietly walked away.
As if searching for hidden warmth,
I shoved my hands
deeply into my pockets,
wondering where time had gone,
wondering what our time had meant,
wondering where my life
was headed now.
I only knew for sure
that tossing the stem into the water
was representative
of letting go and healing,
and beginning all over again

I Could Not Say For Sure

She asked me how I was,
and I replied
that I could not say for sure;
she asked me where I had been,
and I replied
that I could not say for sure;
she asked me what I had been doing,
and I replied
that I could not say for sure;
she asked me where I was going,
and I replied
that I could not say for sure;
she asked me what I was going to do,
and I replied
that I could not say for sure;
she asked me if I was going to be alright,
and I replied
that I could not say for sure;
she asked me if I minded her joining me,
and I replied
that I could not say for sure.
She apprehensively sat down beside me,
took my hand to squeeze it gently,
and leaned her head onto my shoulder
as she whispered that I would be alright.
Suddenly, I could say for sure
that I believed her,
that I believed I would be alright

Future Of The Peaceful Hills

As I look at the hills about me,
they look relaxed and comfortable,
and I begin thinking
about the subtle changes
that I have seen in them
during my meager lifetime.
I cannot help but wonder
how they will weather
the changes facing them
after I have used up my time
here in the valley.
I can only hope
that the next tenant
would give them as many years
of peace and rest
as I have given them,
and pass them on
to the next tenant
in even better shape,
and so on,
and so on,
and so on

Working For Our Treats

The extent of treats
for me and my siblings
during our youth
was normally dependent upon
how many unchipped, unbroken,
popular-brand soda bottles
that we could find
in the ditches along the road.
Each find promised us two cents
when redeemed
at the nearby country store.
If the locals had been drinking enough sodas,
and their aim was not careless
when pitching the bottle out the car window,
and no one else
had already scavenged our territory,
we would likely be able
to collect enough empty bottles
to redeem for candy, sodas, and ice cream.
Yes, those were the good 'ole days,
specially molded for unspoiled children
eager to work for their treats

Peewee

Peewee was a legend in our area,
and many from far and near
recognized his presence on the road
as he played his harmonica
or strummed his guitar and sang,
all the while walking along
at a swift pace that few could match.
His place for the night would be
wherever the wayward wind
had taken him that day,
or wherever he was kindly offered
a place to rest his head.
Often, he would stay
with family, friends, or relatives
until he had worn out his welcome,
but it was always time to move on
if work for his keep was suggested.
He was never very partial to work,
and few could blame him
because he so loved
singing and playing his music.
I never understood his way of life
that seemed to make him happy
for so many years,
but he apparently understood it well.
I love and miss this legend, Peewee,
my oldest sibling,
who had taken a liking to roaming
the highways and byways
before I even drew my first breath

Fred And His Bank

At the small-town local bank,
it used to be the rule,
rather than the exception,
to borrow money on one's word,
but Fred changed that at his bank.
Fred seemed to trust no one,
including me,
just when I was starting to get
an honest start in life.
Because of his personal beliefs,
Fred refused to finance a loan to me
on several occasions,
but I politely informed him each time
that I would get the loan somewhere,
which I obviously did.
I succeeded with my endeavors,
despite the roadblocks
that Fred attempted to put before me.
Unfortunately, he allowed
the actions of the dishonest
to discredit the actions of the honest.
I am certain that Fred never realized
that he and his bank, not I,
were the real losers,
and that he let a good one get away.
However, I certainly realized it,
and I have remembered it vividly
ever since,
by choosing loyalty to other banks
that better understand honesty

The Lowly Dandelion

Because I understand
that which is yet to come,
I can barely abide
the hardy dandelion
during its yellow stage.
I lose all tolerance for it
during its white stage,
just cringing
as I watch the wind
indiscriminately scatter
thousands of its seeds,
which is simply
factual declaration to all
that the dandelion
will always be with us.
There has to be some good
to the wretched weed,
but I just do not know
what that good is.
If I ever do find out,
I still feel quite certain
that my lowly opinion of it
will never be overturned

She Is Beautiful To Someone

Even if she does not believe
that she is beautiful,
she should realize
that somehow,
sometime,
somewhere,
someone will think
that she is beautiful.
She should always
put her best foot forward
and ever be ready
for that wonderful day
when that special someone
recognizes her beauty
and gets enough courage
to tell her so.
What a lovely day
that promises to be,
for the beautiful,
and he who recognizes
the beautiful

The Farmer's Job

As the ground turns green,
and the days get slightly warmer,
the farmer begins getting anxious
to get out into his fields,
but as a Midwest farmer,
he knows
that he must show patience
before putting seeds into the ground.
The ground must be just dry enough
to work up properly,
it must be done
between unpredictable rains,
and it must be done
after the last killing frost.
As much as I respect this man,
and as much as I love the soil,
I am simply not such a gambler.
I do not envy his job at all;
therefore, I will merely admire
and monitor his work from afar
while he continues
putting his livelihood at risk
actively engaging in it

Similarities And Differences

I always wanted
to be like my father,
though his commonness
did not let him shine enough
to catch the eye of many.
Even so,
his honesty and work ethics
outshone those of most,
and there was a light
and sureness about him
that I aspired to emulate.
Although our similarities
were deep and many,
our characteristics showed
yet enough differences
that it was fine
with the both of us
to merely enjoy
our similarities
and effortlessly tolerate
our differences

Destroying Their Beauty

Because my yard
is more than just a yard,
it gets just enough attention
to avoid getting
too much outsider attention.
It plays host
to much more than grass,
including a variety
of much-admired,
tiny, beautiful, wild violets.
Understandably,
it is with great pain, guilt,
and possible regret,
that I simply destroy the beauty
of those delicate violets
with harsh, destructive blades,
all in the name
of doing my duty
to avoid getting
too much outsider attention

No Room For Complacency

The vast expanse
of mountain ranges
lying below
reminds me
how small
and insignificant
we really are
on this journey of life.
During this quiet,
tranquil,
reflective moment,
I am also reminded
that neither is there
room for complacency
from any
on this same journey

Dwell And Play Well

It may be well
to remember
that life continues
even while one chooses
to dwell and play.
It may be equally well
to remember
that life continues
even while one chooses
to neglect
dwell and play.
Accordingly,
it may be well
to remember
that too much
dwell and play
may lead
to missed opportunity
for excelling in life,
and too little
dwell and play
may lead
to missed opportunity
for enjoying life.
So, dwell well,
play well,
excel well,
and enjoy well,
all in wise proportion

My Love For Love

My love for love
has carried me
through many times
when there did not seem
to be much love available,
so that is why
I have thoughtfully pledged
my continuing,
undying loyalty
to my love for love

The Piggy-Back Rides

I miss those piggy-back rides
that I gave my daughter
when she was a child.
Even though
I had to squeeze them in
between work, chores, rest,
and a hundred other
unscheduled, life-filling things,
I tried to not complain
even when
the requests for more
just kept coming.
I well-remember
my own piggy-back rides
when I was a child,
and now that she is grown up,
I wonder
if her piggy-back rides
still reside in her adult heart,
as much as
they resided in her child heart

Replicating Footprints

Our footprints
on the sandy beach
may be closely emulated,
but never exactly replicated,
by others.
Neither can we
replicate the footprints
of others,
or even repeat
our own footprints
just as they are made today.
Such is the way
we should view our own life,
and live it daily
of, by, and for,
our own reasonable sanction
and satisfaction

Expensive Sunglasses

Even though I was prodded
into believing
that I would not be sorry
for my impulsive decision,
it was extremely difficult
for me to part
with the required dollars
to purchase
the expensive sunglasses.
Styling aside,
my world as seen
through my new shades
has been immensely
and smartly enhanced
by any estimation.
Even though I keep expecting
to experience regret
each time I slip them on,
I have yet
to objectively condemn
their questionable acquisition

Our World Stopped
To Take Notice

As my mother lay dying,
my father and I
held her unmoving hands
and watched her breathing
grow more shallow
by the minute,
until it ceased entirely.
As our tired hearts
became even heavier,
we thought
that the world would stop
to take notice,
but to our surprise,
it continued right on
without her.
There was nothing left
for us to do
but drive home in sad silence,
thinking about
what our own world
was going to be like
without her in it anymore.
This was now time,
real time,
when our own world stopped
to take notice,
but the rest of the world
continued

Heart Leading Home

One should
listen closely
and very carefully
to their heart,
without prejudice,
and it will eventually
lead them home,
where it has
wanted to be
all the while,
wherever that is

Sea Waves

Swelled with
lofty confidence,
the open sea
comes gliding
toward shore,
wave after wave
after wave.
Suddenly finding itself
with nowhere to go,
it splashes abruptly
against the sand
with bruised ego,
then humbly disperses

Taking Problems To The Grave

What problems to be solved
would I carry with me
to my grave,
when I could not
or would not
solve them
while I was living?
Who would then take them
from my grave
and solve them
with efficiency,
as I could have
and should have
prior to my passing?
I pray that I will have
sufficient foresight
to not leave an excess
of ineptness behind
for others to deal with

Questions And Answers

Between blessings and disasters,
kindness and greed,
love and hate,
compassion and corruption,
I attempt to sort out
how I feel
about the logic of our system
that we must deal with daily.
I find no easy
or right answers,
only questions about fairness.
Were we not given
such powerful resources
of logic, reasoning, and choice,
I could easily dismiss the issues
and lay them to rest
once and for all.
As it is, however,
the questions continue
to badger me,
and follow me,
wherever my mind goes
when it has time
to casually ponder

Exploring The Mysteries

Exploration of the unknown
and mysterious
comes in small, baby steps
over time too long
for us to comprehend.
Secrets held within
may be revealed to us
in unmeasured, due time,
after countless, bold souls
donate or lend
their life to science,
knowingly by consent,
or after countless,
unsuspecting souls
relinquish the same,
unknowingly
without consent,
all of course
for our own good,
to be divulged
in unmeasured, due time

Our Influences

Even those who have
influenced many others
are influenced,
or have been influenced,
by someone,
because that is how
we learn
and develop
interests and passions.
That is also why
we should be careful
to always set
a good example for others.
At any given time,
someone could be
watching us carefully,
just waiting to follow
and pattern our ways,
good or bad,
positive or negative.
Certainly, all of us
will influence someone;
therefore, let the best in us
shine brightly as a beacon,
and let the worst in us
fade into obscurity

Realistic Recipe For Accomplishments

Past generations
appeared to be light on self-esteem
and self-confidence;
however, imposed expectations
were more moderate then,
so acceptance of accomplishments
were more generous.
The present, developing generation
appears to be heavy on self-esteem
and self-confidence;
however, imposed expectations
are more excessive now,
so acceptance of accomplishments
are less generous.
The sensible would choose a recipe
that is realistic for those behind them,
one that yields
neither excessive self-esteem
and over-confidence,
nor low self-esteem
and under-confidence,
one that yields
neither a false sense of success
and over-accomplishment,
nor a denouncing sense of failure
and under-accomplishment.
After all, a healthy environment
for personal growth and accomplishments
resides more in a foundation of truth
than in a foundation of fantasy

Passion For Life In Spring

As May approaches,
the meadow grasses
deepen their green
and show a strength
impossible to subdue.
Such is the astounding
power of spring,
when passion for life
becomes so strong
that it surges forward
with giant strides
to encourage everyone
and everything
to get active again

Dismay And Tolerance

As much as I dislike
the unbearable cold of winter,
the slightly more-tolerable
heat of summer,
and the constant unpredictability
of everything in between,
I still depend upon
the changing seasons
to keep me honest
and attuned with life.
So, for now, I will attempt
to minimize my dismay,
continue to work on my tolerance,
and resume keeping myself honest
and attuned with life
while dreaming of utopia elsewhere

Night Made For Dancing

Whenever the stars,
full moon,
and mild, pleasant night
get together,
it is a special occasion,
one made for dancing
by those in love.
Should either
tire of dancing,
they can just hold hands
and sit to enjoy
the lovely, enchanting sky
above them,
and let their hearts
do the dancing

The Creek's Soothing Lullaby

When evening falls,
the day sounds
drift off to sleep
and allow me
to fully enjoy
the unbroken trickle
of the spring creek,
and I often use
its soothing lullaby
to examine my day,
and think about
similar beauty
which I may explore
tomorrow

Happy Clouds

The plump,
angel-white clouds
lie lightly afloat
in the deep-blue sky,
looking happy enough
to be jumped on
by playful children,
and any who would not
agree with me
need to spend more time
admiring them
during their charming,
lazy spells
like today

Lilac Bushes At
The Spring Show

Next up will be the lilac bushes,
ready and willing
to show us what they have
here at the spring show.
Their lovely, lavender blossoms
always plead to be gathered
for a table bouquet,
and their elegant, lavish fragrance
always strives to remind us
of all things heavenly.
I already have a good seat,
and I can hardly wait
for their performance to begin

Freedom From Work

Accumulated work
needing to be done
is normally
in direct proportion
to how many things I have.
After too many years
of too many things
and too much, endless work,
I look forward to someday
embracing the day
when I have
but the shirt upon my back.
Maybe then,
I might have
guiltless freedom
to do as I please
each and every day,
that is,
until age and poor health
would remind me
that I need to acquire
more things of comfort

The Angry River

Like an angry snake
pursuing prey,
the dirty river swells
and rises slowly,
sweeping everything in its path
as it rages downstream.
Those able to elude its terror
stand aside and watch
as their dreams
are carried away
in its anger.
Then comes the long wait
in sad silence,
the wait before going back
to assess the probability
that nothing remains
as it was left.
With fears realized,
they have only to sob
without shame
before addressing the next step
of beginning to plan their life
all over again

Vultures On Welfare

The vultures have no problem
with technology and progress,
because they can
sit down to lunch everyday
with a clean plate
and ready menu.
Were it not for us
constantly interrupting them
while they try to dine in peace,
they would surely
consider themselves
extremely fortunate
to be on permanent welfare

Rose-Admiring Time

I was greeted outside today
by blushing rose bushes
laden with beauty.
Although my day
had already been
spoken for,
I reprioritized my agenda
to include
some rose-admiring time.
Later in the evening
when my contentedness
was quite evident,
I surmised that my day
had been well apportioned,
enriched with
extraordinary beauty
that might have been
only common beauty
if not for
my rose-admiring time

Beauty In Sounds

Long ago, I discovered
that there is unique beauty
in sounds,
even when the sources
are not readily evident.
Some of my best walks
have been in darkness
when few are competing
for the beauty around them.
Thus, I carry no guilt
that I am depriving others
if I should gather a surplus
of this mostly unused beauty

Nearly Within The Heavens

As dawn neared,
my anticipation was building
that I might get to see
a rare glimpse
of the cloudless heavens
from this special place.
As darkness finally began
slowly and quietly
waning away,
I suddenly understood
the privilege of standing here
in this high elevation
without clutter
and junk obtrusions in the sky.
Indeed, I seemed to be
nearly within the heavens,
witness to one of the most
serene, pristine views possible
of those heavens
while still standing
here on earth

Calculated Flirtation

Like an excited,
adolescent girl
just discovering
her blossoming beauty
and unable to contain
her will to show it off,
the butterfly
flits lightly about,
dancing and gliding
with calculated flirtation
for any standing by
with a watchful eye

Blocking The Sun

The ominous, devious
winter clouds
slowly gather
to hold hands
and block out the sun,
playing games with us
to further dampen
our dreary moods.
We are merely at a loss
about what to do,
except endure it,
until they
abandon their game
with empathy
and return home

Not One Can Doubt

No, not one,
can doubt
the presence
and power
of His contributing love
when their own,
personal utopia
finally arrives
in spectacular fashion.
No, not even one,
unless their way
is wholly damaged
and irreparable

Greatness Within Us

All have greatness
within them,
and the ones
whom we presently
recognize as great
are merely the ones
who have discovered it
within themselves,
developed it,
nurtured it,
and showed it to others
so that it could be duly
and rightfully recognized

Before I Had The Chance

I seldom read the words
of the well-known poets,
because doing so
tends to influence me
into thinking and writing
like them.
Furthermore,
I get highly irritated
when I realize
that they have utilized
my personal ideas
and written about them
decades or centuries
before I even had
the chance to do so

The Sky's Sunday-Best

I can see that the sky
is tight-lipped today
and has little to say.
Because she is not wearing
her Sunday-best,
maybe she is just sulking
because few
are paying attention to her.
I can put up with
her impetuous pouting
if it is brief,
so long as she continues
to occasionally don
her Sunday-best,
even if it is not Sunday

Trying To Make Love Grow

Those really in love
have reason to be happy,
but everyone
cannot be so fortunate
for many varied reasons,
including bad choices.
Those clinging to love
must try to tolerate
a little unhappiness
and do their best
to make love grow stronger,
setting the tone
for the other to do likewise.
Then, if love shows
no signs of happiness,
they must learn
to either live with it
as best they can,
or not live with it,
and just move on.
Either way,
personal wishes aside,
it shows
overall strength and growth,
howbeit difficult

No Need For Cosmetics

Ms. Nature
has no need for cosmetics;
she is naturally beautiful
just the way she is.
We would know this
if we would only
leave her alone
and judge her
as she is,
not how we want her to be

All Is Not Lost

The spring field of bright yellow
complements the lush green
randomly mixed within it.
This scene of wonder
against the trees coming alive
along the river
makes my heart pause
to take it all in.
Although only a byproduct
of our expanding,
farming literacy,
I am moved to hope
that all is not lost
with our present ways,
and I am also hoping
that the field feels the same

Our Hearts Beat Together

The pulse of our hearts
beats smoothly as one,
and that is why
we have spent
nearly all
of our acquainted life
holding hands.
Occasionally, one will
squeeze the other's hand,
and that reassures both of us
that we are content
to be on the same page,
that we have held steady
during demanding times,
and that we have not
become deterred
getting to where we are,
Ms. Nature and I

Turning Fresh Soil

Few actually turn over
fresh soil anymore,
to let her own nutrients
nourish the crops.
They just loosen and aerate
the soil as it lies,
and then apply
our own artificial,
controversial nutrients
to get the best return
for their investment.
I miss the smell and comfort
of freshly-turned soil,
which used to trigger in me
the certainty
that a new year of growth
was about to begin

Sitting On A Country Porch

There is something
all-soothing and comfortable
about one sitting
on a country porch
to relax and quietly wait
for the evening's darkness
to take them inside,
all the while helping them
diminish their day's troubles
and helping them
form a subtle new hope
and outlook
for tomorrow's agenda

What I Would Give

What I would give
to return to my youth for a day,
to grade new roads in the dry dirt
beneath the big cedar tree
in our front yard;
to push my rusty toy truck
in those newly-created dirt roads
and create the sounds of downshifting
to make it pull harder;
to play with my siblings
until I was hot, sweaty, and worn out;
to go into our huge brick house
and quench my thirst from the dipper
resting in the bucket
of fresh well water;
to go back outside and play
until I was worn out all over again;
to have supper at our large table,
eating our cornbread and milk
while trying to get in a word edgewise
as all excitedly talk about their day;
to gather in our living room
and listen to 'The Lone Ranger' on radio;
to finish the day tired
and jump into the small, lumpy bed
shared with my brother
and fall to sleep in minutes
on the uncomfortable mattress;
to live a day without a care in the world.
What I would give...

Informed Or Not

Glued to televisions or cell phones
in a world
of watching the daily news
filled with crime, hate, and death
cannot be better
than being in a world
of retiring early with the chickens
and getting up with the chickens,
even if the latter choice
is done with blatant blinders.
The dismal knowledge
of those in the former world,
or the dismal lack of knowledge
of those in the latter world,
will likely make little difference
in the future outcome
facing all of us

A Touch Of Softness

The cluster
of beautiful purple irises
gives me
a touch of softness
as I leave for the day,
and they promise
to make me
a more forgiving,
more tolerant person,
and a more pleasant
person to be around,
which is why
I continue
to admire their beauty
at every opportunity

The Plain Country Church

Their voices
do not blend very well
as their songs echo
from within the plain,
one-room country church,
but they are not there
to impress others,
bur rather to praise Him
in the best way
they know how.
As I saunter along
vaguely processing
the wonderful,
hideous singing
on this peaceful
Sunday morning,
I feel His warm presence,
and I am humbly impressed
that they do not
feel the need to impress

Mountain Man In Spirit

He was born a century
and a half too late,
this reserved man
who would much rather be
a mountain man.
He feels at home
in his deerskin clothing,
moccasins, and beaver hat,
wears his favorite knife
comfortably at his sash,
and carries his flintlock rifle,
powder horn, and possibles bag
like the treasures and necessities
they were in times past.
Realistically, he knows
that he will never engage
his knife or rifle
to save his own life
or put food on the table,
but he prides himself in knowing
that he could if he had to.
On this fall day of getting away
in the rugged hills
that freely talk with him,
he is at peace dreaming
of those perilous, coveted days
that he never saw,
and likely never will see

Survivors And Enjoyers

We are made to be
survivors primarily
and enjoyers secondly,
but it seems like
such a waste
for us to spend our lives
merely surviving
on a day-to-day basis.
The fortunate
will find a means
of tipping the scale
toward enjoyment,
while the unfortunate
must continue
dealing with
the scale tipped
toward mere survival

Extracting Loveliness From Life

I certainly do not profess
to have a corner
on extracting
loveliness from life,
but I do profess
to have been
somewhat successful at it;
furthermore, I intend
to adamantly continue
trying to get
even better at it,
so long as life remains
within me

Sharing Beauty

The white, homemade,
wooden box
below her front window
is seasonably filled
with a mix
of colorful,
homegrown flowers,
which is just
her way of saying
that she enjoys
nurturing beauty,
and that she merely
enjoys passing it on
by sharing it with others

Forwarding Hope

The gentle spring rain
manages to come
just when
it is supposed to come,
forwarding some hope
for normalcy
regarding crops,
life,
prosperity,
and happiness,
in that order

Happy Where She Is

The word about
is that her adult children
are not helping her
during her aging years,
that she must clean her own house
and cook her own food.
Worst of all, they say,
is that she still must raise
her own garden for food,
but then she must give most of it
to her own children.
They wonder why her children
do not insist that she move into town,
but I know why,
because I understand her,
just as her children understand her.
She is where she wants to be.
She feels tidy
when her linoleum-covered floors
have been swept with her broom,
she feels satisfied after eating
her own home-cooked meals,
and she feels needed
when she shares her garden-raised produce
with her children.
Most of all,
she feels at-home, peaceful, and happy
where she is,
and that is reason enough for her children
to let her stay there, with their blessings

Passing On Happiness

When I have exhausted
my quest
to experience
every kind of happiness
that life offers,
it is time to take me
to the other side
and give my space
to another.
However, I have yet
to figure out
a viable way of passing on
my accrued happiness,
so that it is not lost,
and wasted,
after I have gone

Newcomer To The Neighborhood

The tiny sweet wildflower
must be bold, indeed,
to set down roots
in a place so foreign to her.
Even though I believe
that her new residence
will suit her just fine,
she did stand out enough
that I noticed her,
and others may
question her presence
as well.
However, she has
nothing to fear from me,
because I welcome
all newcomers
to the neighborhood,
and I will be her friend
even if others
do not accept her

In My Pursuit Of Life

Not so many years ago,
I went everywhere at a run
because I was searching
for my place in life
by pursuing
all available avenues.
I have since found my place,
and I have learned much
along the way in finding it.
I have been privileged
to apply a handsome portion
of that which I learned,
but I have yet
more places to see
and more beauty to witness
before I am content
to be finished.
I can only hope
that I am truly finished
pursuing life
by the time
death has finished
pursuing me

About The Author

Jim was born in Metamora, Indiana, in 1949, and has lived most of his life there. He was the youngest of eleven children and was raised on a 175-acre farm. From an early age, everyone in the family was expected to keep up their chores necessary to raise food and crops for their winter survival and paying the mortgage. Work time held a higher priority than playtime, but time for play was always squeezed in when possible. His roots exploring nature on the farm proved to be a very memorable and influential part of his life. His father worked the small farm, but the limited, tillable land was not exactly conducive to a prosperous living. His mother worked outside the home as the last of the children were born. The family was poor, but they realized many years later that they experienced a good life on the farm.

Jim grew up quite reserved. Only when complimented and encouraged by his eighth-grade teacher at Metamora, did he realize that he might have a little potential. Brookville High School was a big adjustment for him, even though it was relatively small compared to today's consolidations. Adjusting to high school was a difficult social adjustment, but he had very good success academically. Burying himself in books was much easier than engaging in sports and other social activities.

He attended Ivy Tech Community College and began working at Cummins Engine Company in Columbus, Indiana, in 1968. He continued his education with night classes for nearly four years. Little did he know that he would work at Cummins for 32 years. It was a different time when employees were loyal to employers, and employers highly valued their employees. The economy was mostly booming in the late sixties, but the diesel engine business didn't necessarily follow the general trends of the economy. Many of the years there were prosperous, but there were many lean years as well, when all were expected to sacrifice for the company's survival. All his years at Cummins were spent in engineering drafting design, where he discovered his perfectionist traits. It seemed to suit him well when he became heavily involved in diesel engine fuel systems, working daily with precise drawing tolerances and specifications.

Jim married in 1972 and lived in Columbus for a short time. However, the decision was made to move back to Metamora just before their daughter was born in 1977. While employed at Cummins, he acquired several hundred acres of land in the same valley where he had grown up. Forty acres of that were part of the family farm, making him the third-generation owner since 1921. He felt a self-imposed obligation to his father to dabble in farming, but soon discovered that it was basically a full-time job with only meager results at best.

He eventually decided that it was enough to merely own and love the land, rather than attempt to farm it.

In 1978, Jim discovered running, and that has had a big impact on his life. His dream of running the Boston Marathon was realized in 1983 and 1984 when he was heavily competing in races. In 1984, he did high-mileage training by running nearly 4700 miles, averaging 90 miles per week, which resulted in his most competitive year of racing. However, he suffered a broken knee in a 1985 car accident, the worst prognosis for an aspiring, highly-motivated runner. After that, he never fully regained his prior level of motivation and drive to compete at a high level. He now runs three miles every day to stay healthy, with a lifetime running tally of over 47,000 miles.

Jim divorced in 1994, and then concentrated on getting his daughter through college. Retiring in 2000, at age 51, he finally experienced some welcomed time for hobbies and leisure. He met his future wife in 1998, and they married in 2005. They presently reside in Shelbyville, Indiana.

As most eventually discover, there comes a time in one's life when it becomes logical to downsize. Some of the hardest decisions of Jim's life came in 2004, and again in 2015, when he decided that it was time to part with some of his beloved land. It was someone else's turn to be the steward for the valley that he had owned for so long; however, he still retains the forty acres from the family farm. Jim easily has enough interests and hobbies to keep him busy until he reaches a hundred years of age, which remains his goal if his health cooperates. He is still very passionate about his writing, consistently finding inspiration to further his works.

Lightning Source UK Ltd.
Milton Keynes UK
UKHW021143040821
388300UK00013B/647